Wait! Before You Head for the Mountaintop...

You may be skeptical about kids making treats for t
Believe it or not, they can do it...and they'll have *loa*
others! In field tests, even preschoolers were able to make snack in the allotted time. Before you decide to make alternative snack arrangements, consider the following reminders:

- ▲ Follow the setup and preparation instructions in this manual. Remember, the recipes have been field-tested and revised for quick and easy snack making.
- ▲ It's okay if kids' treats don't look perfect. The hungry kids who visit Mountaintop Treats each day won't even notice. They'll love that their friends made the treats!
- ▲ You're giving kids a chance to experience the joy in serving—a *valuable* life lesson.

Basic Things You Need to Know

- ▲ **Understand how Everest VBS works.** The kids at Everest VBS rotate through stations in small, mixed-age groups of five, called Climbing Crews, with an adult or teenage Crew Leader. Every day one-fourth of the Crews skip Glacier Games to make snacks for everyone at VBS. Kids go to the opening Base Camp Sing & Play first, so you'll have approximately 20 minutes for preparation before the snack service Crews arrive. There's one more 20-minute rotation *after* snack preparation (before all the kids arrive to eat the snacks), so you and your kitchen crew can use that time to finish anything that wasn't completed by the snack service Crews. Remaining prep work can vary from day to day, so it's nice to have that cushion of time!
- ▲ **Get a kitchen crew.** Your Everest VBS Director will ask a few volunteers to assist you during the week. This kitchen crew can help you set up tables, set out supplies, make quick trips to the store if necessary, and clean up after the snack rotation. Be sure to let your kitchen crew know that this is an opportunity for the *kids* to experience a spirit of service as they work with their Crews to make the snacks.
- ▲ **Involve Crew Leaders.** Crew Leaders will help ensure that Crew members clean their hands (using hand wipes or antibacterial gel) before starting snack preparation. They'll help guide the kids in adding the appropriate amount of ingredients to each snack. Crew Leaders can also help pour or serve the water during snack time. If Crews finish making the snack before the rotation is over, Crew Leaders can guide discussions about what everyone is learning at Everest VBS.

"Hold on!"

- ▲ **Use the Bible Point.** Every activity at Everest focuses on one simple, memorable Bible truth called the Bible Point. Kids will be listening for the Bible Point so they can shout "Hold on!" Each time kids shout "Hold on!" they'll grasp their forearms in front of themselves. (See photo.)
- ▲ **Explain how the treats reinforce the Bible verse.** When kids arrive to make snacks, you'll give a brief explanation of how the snack ties to the day's key Bible verse. It's important to use a sound system in your snack area so everyone can hear you. A photocopiable "Today's Mountaintop Treat" snack explanation is included in each day's lesson to place on snack trays for each Crew Leader. Crew Leaders can discuss the Bible connection during snack time and use the Bible Buddy app to bring the daily Bible focus to life!

vbsbuddies.com

Be sure to download the fun, *free* Bible Buddy app! Keywords: Everest Bible Memory Buddies

Available on the App Store | Android App on Google play

- ▲ **Use an attention-getting signal.** Using the Yak Bell or another noisemaker lets kids know when it's time to stop what they're doing and give you their attention. Ask your Everest VBS Director about having a fun Yak Bell (available from Group Publishing) at Mountaintop Treats.
- ▲ **Include preschoolers.** We've learned that having preschoolers make the snack on the first day sets the tone for the week. Kids see that even little ones can serve and share Jesus' love. It also sets skeptical adults at ease; when they see that preschoolers can do this, they'll realize that the rest of the week will be a snap.
- ▲ **Congratulate and celebrate your servers.** Climbing Crews are identified by name or number. Find out which Crews are serving each day so you can be sure to invite them up front at snack time and have everyone give a rousing cheer!

On the final day of Everest VBS, ask your kitchen crew to come forward so kids can show their appreciation for these hardworking volunteers, too!

- **Be aware of allergies.** Be sure to check the registration lists to find out if you have participants with food allergies. Usually some parts of the snack are okay for them to eat, and we've done our best to be mindful of the more common allergies. We've also included suggestions for alternative ingredients in snacks to make them gluten-free or dairy-free. Be aware that some food is made in a factory that also processes nuts; check the package to find this information. If a child has severe or numerous allergies, the Director might ask the parent to bring an appropriate snack each day.
- **Have your kitchen crew prepare the alternate snack trays.** If there are participants who have food allergies, have your kitchen crew prepare the trays for those Climbing Crews, using the same alternative ingredients for all the snacks on those trays, to minimize the risk of a child getting a snack that could cause a harmful reaction. (Since the kitchen crew is preparing trays for those Crews, subtract that number of participants from the number you use to divide supplies for the service crew prep tables.)
- **Write the Crew number on the Crew Leader's "Today's Mountaintop Treat" handout for each tray with the alternate snacks.** During snack time, your kitchen crew can deliver these special trays to the correct Crews. Ask the VBS Director to make an announcement during the Base Camp Sing & Play Day 1 huddle and prayer time with Crew Leaders about how you'll handle delivering trays to Crews that have kids with food allergies so the leaders of those Crews know the process.

Setting Up Mountaintop Treats

- **Choose locations for snack prep and dining.** If you can't use the same area for both activities, it's a good idea to use areas that are close together. If your prep area is carpeted, consider taping inexpensive plastic table covers on the floor under each prep table to protect from inevitable spills. Eating outdoors in a *shaded* area is great when the weather is nice. Crews can spread out, and it's easier to hear each other as they talk during snack time.
- **Set up a prep table for each snack service Crew.** Be sure there's room between tables for Crew members to work. You might also need counter space or extra tables to place the completed trays of snacks and the cups and pitchers of water. Carts can come in handy if you're moving snack tray items from the prep area to another location. Be sure to supply hand wipes and paper towels for each Crew to clean their hands before starting to make the snacks, and they'll probably use plenty during the snack creation process, too!
- **Get a count.** At the beginning of each day, check with the registration helpers to find out how many kids checked in for that day. Add extra for Crew Leaders, Station Leaders, and other staff. Divide the total number of people by the number of preparation tables, and stock each table with that number of snack plates or cups, ingredients, and other supplies. (Subtract the number of Crews that have kids with allergies.) Snack service Crews will know that when they've completed their number of plates or resealable bags, they're done!
- **Use a microphone and speaker.** It definitely gets noisy at snack time, so you'll want to make sure everyone can hear your snack explanation and instructions.
- **Have Crews gather on mats.** If kids are eating indoors, set out washable mats or blankets for Crews to sit on. This helps keep the floor from getting too dirty or sticky. Even if everyone is eating outdoors, using mats or blankets helps keep Crews together for discussion while they're enjoying snack. Plus, if you set out a mat for every Crew, you'll know if everyone has arrived or not by simply seeing that all the mats are taken!
- **Turn your snack area into an icy Everest scene!** If you're indoors, cover walls with the Snowscape or Winter Sky Plastic Backdrops. Drape a Gleam 'N Curtain in the doorway, and string paper snowflakes and Lightcicles from the ceiling. If you're outdoors, consider setting up pop-up canopies for shade. Create fun directional signs that say things such as "Base Camp Survival Food," and hang up the Mountaintop Treats station sign. You'll find many of these decorating items in your Everest VBS catalog, or brainstorm via Facebook at facebook.com/groupvbs.

Mountaintop Treats Poster

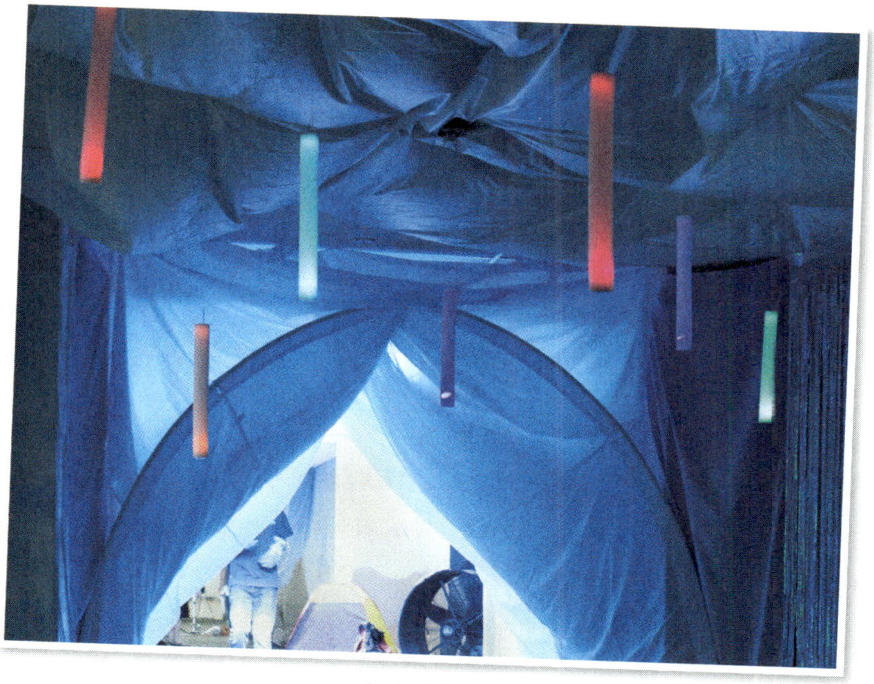
Lightcicles

Every day you'll use...

Purchase these:

- ▲ wet wipes (1 box per prep table plus an extra box or two for snack time)
- ▲ paper towels (1 roll per prep table)
- ▲ paper table covers (1 per prep table per day, optional)
- ▲ napkins (1 per participant per day)
- ▲ drinking cups (1 per participant per day)
- ▲ Yak Bell* or other attention-getter

*available from Group Publishing or your Group VBS supplier

Round up these:

- ▲ Bible
- ▲ water pitchers
- ▲ sturdy serving trays (1 per Climbing Crew)—can also use baking sheets
- ▲ prep tables (1 per prep Crew)
- ▲ microphone and speaker—highly recommended
- ▲ washable mats or blankets (1 per Climbing Crew)—optional, for Crews to sit on during snack
- ▲ large trash cans or trash bags

Supply Lists

You'll find a complete list of Mountaintop Treats supplies in the Master Supply List at group.com/vbsTools; in addition, the supplies for each day are listed in this manual. You probably won't have to purchase everything from your VBS budget. Many congregation members are happy to donate money or food items; use the handy photocopiable snack donation request form, found on the *Everest Clip Art & Resources* CD, to let them know how they can help. Check your church kitchen to see what serving supplies and paper goods are available for your use. See if you can borrow things like serving trays or mixing bowls if you don't have enough at your church.

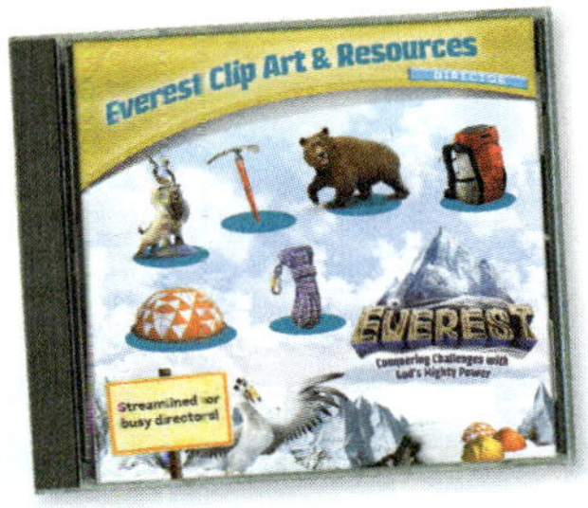

DAY 1

Bible Story: God provides for Elijah. (1 Kings 17)

Bible Point: God has the power to provide.

Key Verse: "And God will generously provide all you need." (2 Corinthians 9:8)

Did You Know?

- Elijah was a prophet in Israel during the rule of King Ahab, whose reign is placed around 874-853 B.C. Elijah called for people, specifically the rulers of Israel and Judah, to put their faith in God rather than the false god Baal.
- Elijah's name means "my God is Yahweh." *Yahweh,* meaning "Lord," is the Hebrew word for God. Another way to phrase it is "the Lord is my God." Even Elijah's name reminded God's people to repent and once again worship God.
- Elijah spread his message about God throughout the capital and major cities of the kingdom. The Bible says Elijah came from a land east of the Jordan River, from a place called Gilead. This means that the urban people Elijah spoke to probably looked down on him, regarding him as a simple, uneducated country man. What a great reminder that God can use anybody to do his work!
- Baal was known as the god of lightning and storm; he was believed to have control over the fertility of the land and crops. God sent a great drought over the land by withholding the rain, showing King Ahab and the people of Israel that Baal had no power.

Why It Matters...

Although most kids at your VBS probably have a place to sleep and food to eat, they still have other real needs—maybe a child's parent lost his or her job, or perhaps a child feels friendless at school. Help children understand that God is bigger than any of those needs, and he has the power to provide. Give kids the reassurance that they can hold on to God's mighty power to provide for their needs. You'll also have the opportunity to encourage kids to recognize and thank God for providing their most fundamental blessings—things like clean drinking water, the privilege of coming to church to learn about Jesus, and love from friends and family members.

At Everest VBS, the daily Bible Point is carefully integrated into each station's activities for unforgettable Bible learning. See how your station reinforces today's Bible Point.

DAY 1

God has the power to provide.

Base Camp Sing & Play

- Learn the Day 1 Bible Point and key verse, and meet Bible Memory Buddy Klymer.
- Sing Everest VBS songs.
- Meet Trek Rockrambler, a world-famous climber whose climbing crew left for Everest without him.

Bible Expeditions

- Drink water from a brook and receive food from ravens and discover that God provides.

Mountaintop Treats

Trail Mix

KidVid™ Cinema

Ukrainian brothers Deacon, Hudson, and Ben needed a family, and God provided in a big way!

Imagination Station

Grow fluffy flakes in a flash with Snow Seeds... and remember how God generously provides!

Summit Celebration

- See who is starring in today's Spotlight VBS.
- Review the day.
- Get the day's Bible Bands to take home.
- Discover the difference between "need" and "want."

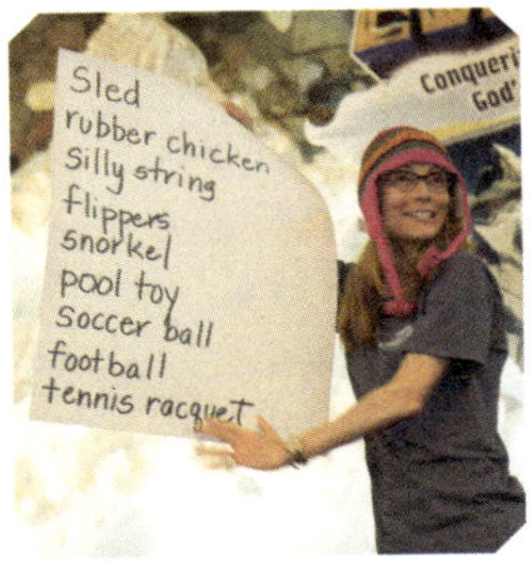

Glacier Games

Ice to Know You

Porter Parade

Everest Relay

Day 1

Supplies

- dried chunk pineapple (about 3 pieces per participant)
- raisins or dried cranberries (about 6 per participant)
- sunflower seeds (2 tablespoons per participant)
- shredded coconut (2 tablespoons per participant)
- banana chips (about 3 per participant)
- mini chocolate chips (2 tablespoons per participant)—optional
- plastic spoons or 3-ounce plastic cups (5 per prep table)—see note in "Before Preschoolers Arrive"
- plastic spoons (1 per participant)
- 9-ounce clear plastic cups (1 per participant)
- large bowls (6 per prep table)
- photocopies of "Today's Mountaintop Treat: Trail Mix" (1 per Crew)

Allergy Alert!

If there are children with food allergies, find out what parts of today's snack are okay for them to eat. Prepare any necessary snack variations or alternatives in advance. For the Crews with allergy alerts, you can prepare those Crews' entire tray with the snack variation to ensure there aren't any mix-ups of who gets what snack and no one feels left out. Be sure to carefully check ingredient lists, as some food is made in facilities that also process peanuts.

Today's Mountaintop Treat—Trail Mix

Preschoolers will make a delicious and healthy trail mix as a reminder that God has the power to provide.

Before Preschoolers Arrive

Fill large bowls with the trail mix ingredients (one bowl for each ingredient) for each prep table. Divide the supplies and place on each table. (If you have trays for Crews with alternative ingredients, subtract that number from the amount of supplies for the prep tables, since the kitchen crew will assemble those trays.)

The supply list shows quantities in tablespoons so you can estimate the amount of ingredients you need to purchase for the number of participants at your VBS. Although we've made suggestions for dried fruits to include in the trail mix, you can choose other options as you wish. Just be mindful to stay away from peanuts and tree nuts for the sake of more common and severe food allergies.

We had preschoolers use plastic spoons instead of actual measuring spoons to scoop ingredients; you could let preschoolers use 3-ounce plastic cups instead of spoons and have them put just one scoop of an ingredient into the snack cups. This might also make it easier for the youngest of your preschoolers to scoop up the dried fruit.

Place the ingredient bowls for each prep table in an assembly line down the center of the table in this order: banana chips, mini chocolate chips, shredded coconut, sunflower seeds, raisins or dried cranberries, dried pineapple chunks. Then place a plastic spoon in each ingredient bowl. Put the 9-ounce cups for each table at the end near the banana chips, as well as wet wipes and paper towels.

It's also necessary to use lower tables so preschoolers can easily reach the ingredients. If you decide to have preschoolers make snacks in the preschool area, you'll need trays or carts to carry the finished treats to your dining area.

Make a snack as an example to show the preschoolers.

Welcome to Snack Service

Greet all the preschoolers, and welcome them to the Mountaintop Treats kitchen. Gather preschool Crews in an area away from the food to explain today's treat.

Say: **Today you have a very special job here at Everest VBS—you get to make today's snack for everyone!** Tell what you like most about making food, and ask a few willing children to tell about a time they've helped a parent or another adult make a tasty treat.

The Bible Connection

Say: **Making yummy treats is a lot of fun, but here at Everest VBS, our treats also help us remember our Bible verse.** Hold up a Bible. **Today we're learning from the Bible—God's *very* special book—that God takes care of us. Our Bible verse from 2 Corinthians 9:8 says: "And God will generously provide all you need." That means God is strong enough to give us things we need, like our families, water, food, and more! God has the power to provide. *(Hold on!)***

Hold up the sample snack. **God made all the plants and animals in the world that help us have food—just like today's snack, called a Trail Mix. Trail Mix is a great treat that gives climbers energy for a climb up Mount Everest.**

Remind kids that the snack is for eating *later*, not right now. Have each snack prep Crew gather around a prep table. Briefly explain to preschoolers and Crew Leaders how they'll assemble the snacks by adding one ingredient at a time to the cups and passing them down their assembly line.

Field Test Finding

During our field test, the assembly line approach to putting the treat together worked great! Each preschooler had something to add to the snack cups. Have your kitchen crew look over the snack cups and add ingredients to any that didn't get about a half cup of trail mix.

Worried about germs? Have children clean their hands thoroughly with wet wipes before and after making the snacks. Crew Leaders can remind their kids to avoid putting fingers in their mouths!

Snack Assembly

1. Have Crew Leaders help preschoolers count 3 banana chips to put in each 9-ounce clear plastic cup as the first layer of the Trail Mix.

2. Let preschoolers use the plastic spoons to scoop 2 portions of mini chocolate chips, shredded coconut, and sunflower seeds—in that order—into each plastic cup.

3. Have Crew Leaders help preschoolers count 6 raisins or dried cranberries and 3 pieces of dried pineapple. Each cup should now have dried pineapple and raisins or dried cranberries on top. The order the dried fruit goes into the cup doesn't matter.

4. Put 6 completed snacks onto each serving tray, along with 6 spoons, 6 napkins, and a copy of "Today's Mountaintop Treat."

Snack Blessing

Lead preschoolers in prayer for the snacks they've just prepared for others at Everest VBS. You could thank God for providing food—like today's snack—that helps us stay alive and healthy, and gives us a good reminder that **God has the power to provide.** ***(Hold on!)***

Snack Time

When all the Climbing Crews have arrived and found a place to sit, sound the Yak Bell (or another loud noisemaker) to get everyone's attention. Welcome the Crews to Mountaintop Treats, and tell them that the preschoolers prepared today's snack. If preschoolers are eating with the whole group, have all the Thank You-ers lead everyone in cheering for them; otherwise, everyone can thank them when they're gathered again at Base Camp Sing and Play.

For today, since preschoolers are too small to carry the trays, have Crew Leaders invite two willing kids from their Crew to come forward to get a tray of snacks and cups of water for their Crew. Your kitchen crew can deliver any trays prepared for unique allergy or dietary needs.

Say: **God gives us things we need because he loves us *so* much. Sometimes it might feel like we're not getting what we need—kind of like the dried-out fruit on the top of our Trail Mix.** Hold up a piece of dried fruit, and have Crew members tell about a time they had to *really* wait for something they needed. **When we don't have what we need, it can make us sad—even cry tears shaped kind of like the sunflower seeds.** Have kids find a sunflower seed in their snack and examine its shape. **But it doesn't mean God doesn't love us or care about us. God knows the *best* time to give us what we need, and God has the power to provide. *(Hold on!)* When we hold on and wait patiently for God, it's even more wonderful when we get what we need—like the sweet treat at the bottom of our Trail Mix!**

Be sure Crew Leaders have a photocopy of the "Today's Mountaintop Treat" card so they can help kids continue talking about today's Bible focus as they eat their snack.

Remind Crew Leaders to help everyone have clean hands before they eat. Ask the Prayer Persons to lead their Crew in a prayer of thanks for the snack.

Field Test Finding

More like a field test God Sighting! Our preschool Crews happened to be the last to arrive to the Mountaintop Treats area at snack time, and it worked out perfectly. Before the preschoolers arrived, the Station Leader invited all of the other Crews to cheer for the preschoolers as they arrived because they'd prepared the snack. As the preschoolers came into the snack area, they were met with thankful cheers and clapping. Their little faces glowed, and it was a highlight of the day!

Finishing Up

When you hear your VBS Director's signal, ask Crews to help by putting their used cups and napkins in the trash containers. Then dismiss kids to their next station.

Your kitchen crew can help pick up the Crew mats or blankets, wipe up spills (if you're eating indoors), and straighten up the kitchen and snack area before they leave.

Day 1

Today's Mountaintop Treat
Trail Mix

Crew Leader, as kids begin to eat, read aloud today's Bible verse:
"And God will generously provide all you need" (2 Corinthians 9:8).

Help Crew members examine each layer of the snack and tell about times they have felt "dry" or forgotten or sad and had to wait for God to provide—and how they felt when God provided for their needs. Lead with a simple example from your own life to help kids make the connection.

Download the *free* Bible Buddy app! Snack is a great time to bring the Bible focus to life on your smart device!

Available on the App Store | Android App on Google play

Day 1

Today's Mountaintop Treat
Trail Mix

Crew Leader, as kids begin to eat, read aloud today's Bible verse:
"And God will generously provide all you need" (2 Corinthians 9:8).

Help Crew members examine each layer of the snack and tell about times they have felt "dry" or forgotten or sad and had to wait for God to provide—and how they felt when God provided for their needs. Lead with a simple example from your own life to help kids make the connection.

Download the free Bible Buddy app! Snack is a great time to bring the Bible focus to life on your smart device!

Available on the App Store | Android App on Google play

Permission to photocopy this resource from Group's Everest VBS granted for local church use. Copyright © 2015 Group Publishing, Inc., Loveland, CO. group.com/vbs

Bible Story:
God speaks to Elijah.
(1 Kings 19)

Bible Point:
God has the power to comfort.

Key Verse:
"He comforts us in all our troubles so that we can comfort others."
(2 Corinthians 1:4)

DAY 2

Did You Know?

- As Elijah fled from King Ahab and his wife, Jezebel, Elijah hit one of the lowest points in his life—he even told God he had had enough and asked God to end his life! No wonder Elijah desperately needed God's comfort. Jezebel, the powerful queen of Israel, wanted to kill him; he was the *only* prophet in Israel serving God, as Jezebel tried to have all the other prophets of God killed, and the few who were left were in hiding; and even after God had demonstrated his great power, Jezebel *still* wouldn't worship God.
- Before Elijah began his 40-day trek to Mount Sinai, he stopped to rest under a broom tree. The broom tree is common in this desert wilderness (modern-day southern Palestine), and it would have been the only shrub big enough to offer Elijah any shade. The broom tree can grow to be 10 feet high.
- Instead of appearing in the mighty wind, earthquake, or fire, God presented himself in a gentle whisper. Why? God had just shown his great power to the people of Israel by withholding the rain to create a significant drought and by sending down fire to consume the sacrifice offered by Elijah at Mount Carmel (1 Kings 18). But God revealed that he is more than just a powerful God who can control the elements of nature—he is a God who is always present, sometimes revealed in overwhelmingly astounding ways and sometimes in the quiet.

Why It Matters...

Our world is an imperfect place, and it's filled with things that make kids scared or sad or fearful—hurtful words from a child at school, a frightening storm, a fight between parents. Kids find comfort in things like a warm hug, an encouraging word, or a cozy stuffed animal, but nothing compares to the comfort of knowing God is always by their side—they are never alone! Today at VBS share with kids the encouraging message of God's peace and his ability to comfort us no matter what we might face in life.

DAY 2

God has the power to comfort.

At Everest VBS, the daily Bible Point is carefully integrated into each station's activities for unforgettable Bible learning. See how your station reinforces today's Bible Point.

Base Camp Sing & Play

- Learn the Day 2 Bible Point and key verse, and meet Bible Memory Buddy Cliff.
- Sing Everest VBS songs.
- Discuss God Sightings, and hang a God Sightings Flag.
- Trek is sick and in need of some powerful comfort to make him feel better!

Bible Expeditions

- Hide from a windstorm, earthquake, and fire; then be comforted by God's powerful love.

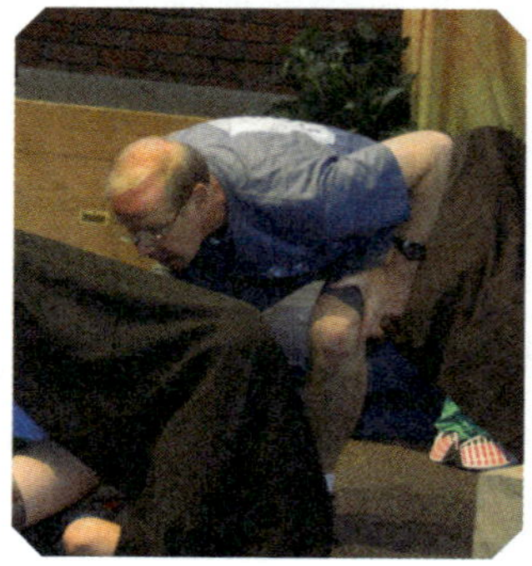

Mountaintop Treats

Rock Rambler's Parfait

KidVid™ Cinema

Twins Ben and Sam share God's love by sewing soft, colorful stuffed monsters for kids who are hurting.

Imagination Station

Create a soft, surprising bubble rope as a reminder of God's comforting power!

Summit Celebration

- Watch for familiar faces in today's Spotlight VBS.
- Review the day.
- Get the day's Bible Bands to take home.
- Learn how God's comfort is overflowing.

Glacier Games

Core Connection

Mountaintop Rescue

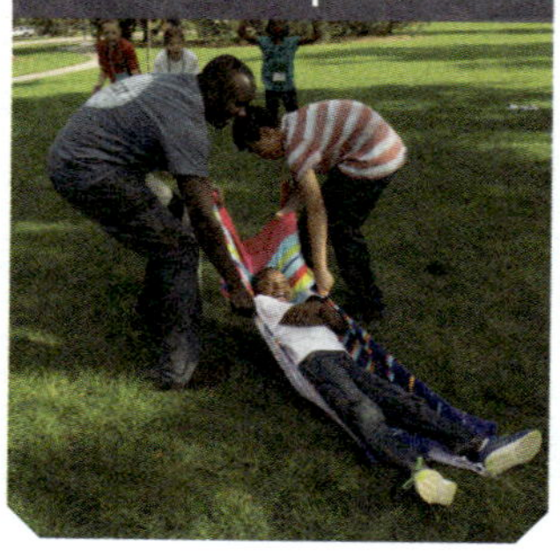

Hold On!

Day 2

Today's Mountaintop Treat—Rock Rambler's Parfait

Today's treat is an awesome reminder that God has the power to comfort and that God's comfort is soft and gentle but also mighty and strong.

Before Snack Service Crews Arrive

Mark five 9-ounce clear plastic cups per prep table with a line that shows a ½ cup measurement (kids will use these as measuring cups during snack assembly):

- ▲ Use your actual measuring cup to pour ½ cup of granola into a 9-ounce plastic cup.
- ▲ Level out the granola, and then on the outside of the plastic cup mark a line at the top of the granola with a permanent marker. This is a ½ cup measuring line.
- ▲ Dump the granola back into its container.
- ▲ Mark the remaining prep table cups with the same ½ cup line as the first, and divide the marked measuring cups among prep tables.

Set out the tubs of yogurt and boxes of granola and prep supplies for each table (or put yogurt and granola in large bowls for easier scooping). Put one pair of child-safe scissors at each prep table. Make sure each prep table has wet wipes and paper towels for hand cleaning. Make a sample completed snack, with the yogurt as the bottom layer and the granola on top.

Supplies

- ▲ strawberry yogurt (½ cup per participant)
- ▲ granola (½ cup per participant)—you can also find gluten-free options in many stores
- ▲ bowls for yogurt and granola (2 per prep table, optional)
- ▲ half-cup measuring cup
- ▲ 9-ounce clear plastic cups marked at ½ cup (5 per prep table)
- ▲ 9-ounce clear plastic cups for the parfait (1 per participant)
- ▲ dark-colored permanent marker
- ▲ spoons (5 per prep table; 1 per participant at snack time)
- ▲ brown paper lunch bags (1 per Crew)
- ▲ child-safe scissors (1 per prep table)
- ▲ photocopies of "Today's Mountaintop Treat: Rock Rambler's Parfait" (1 per Crew)

Allergy Alert!

If there are children with food allergies, find out what parts of today's snack are okay for them to eat. Prepare any necessary snack variations or alternatives in advance. For the Crews with allergy alerts, you can prepare those Crews' entire tray with the snack variation to ensure there aren't any mix-ups of who gets what snack and no one feels left out. Be sure to carefully check ingredient lists, as some food is made in facilities that also process peanuts.

Welcome to Snack Service

After all the snack service Crews have gathered, use the Yak Bell to get their attention, and welcome them to the Mountaintop Treats kitchen.

Say: **Today it's *your* turn to make and serve today's snack!** Invite a few willing kids to share what they like about serving or doing nice things for others. **Serving others is one of the best parts of Mountaintop Treats! Are you ready to get started?**

The Bible Connection

Say: **Each day at Everest VBS, our snack can help us remember our Bible verse. Today's comes from 2 Corinthians 1:4: "He comforts us in all our troubles so that we can comfort others."** Hold up your sample snack so everyone can see it. **This snack is called a Rock Rambler's Parfait!** Ask:

? **Why is serving this snack a way to comfort our friends at Everest VBS?**

Say: **Serving or doing kind things for others is a great way to comfort! The granola in our snack** (point to the granola layer) **kind of looks like strong rocks or boulders. God's comfort is strong, but it's also gentle and even sweet** (point to the yogurt layer). **God has the power to comfort. *(Hold on!)***

Briefly walk your snack service Crews through the snack assembly steps before they begin making today's snack. Kids can choose to scoop granola or yogurt into snack cups or to cut paper bags. Explain that when everyone is assembled at snack time, the snack service Crews will distribute the snack trays to all the Climbing Crews. Crew Leaders or older kids can take cups of water to the Crews.

Trail Tip

If you have many participants with dairy or gluten allergies, you can purchase 5.3-ounce containers of Silk Strawberry Soy Fruity & Creamy yogurt to serve as an alternative. This brand of yogurt is free of lactose, gluten, dairy, casein, egg, MSG, and high-fructose corn syrup. A healthy and yummy, allergy-sensitive option!

Have children clean their hands thoroughly with wet wipes before and after making the snacks. Crew Leaders can remind kids that the snacks are for eating later if the treats start comforting growling stomachs a little too soon!

Snack Assembly

1. Use the marked cups to measure out ½ cup of granola per Crew member into each brown paper bag. Spoon granola up to the marked line on the cups, and then dump the measured amounts into the brown paper bags.

2. After granola is measured into each brown paper lunch bag, cut each bag so the top of the bag is about ½ inch above the granola. (You can use disposable bowls instead of the brown paper lunch bags; the bags give the snack an outdoorsy look.)

3. Spoon a half cup of yogurt from the large containers into each 9-ounce plastic cup. For ease of measuring, set each plain 9-ounce plastic cup inside the marked measuring cup, and add the yogurt up to the ½ cup line. Then remove and set aside the snack cup filled with yogurt.

4. Prepare serving trays for each Climbing Crew at VBS with 6 of the following: spoons, napkins, and 9-ounce cups filled with ½ cup of yogurt. Include a brown paper bag of granola on each tray, along with a copy of "Today's Mountaintop Treat" handout.

Snack Blessing

Have the Prayer Person for each snack service Crew ask God to bless the snacks they've just prepared for others at Everest VBS.

Trail Tip

Prepare each serving tray for the maximum Climbing Crew size at your VBS so each Crew will have enough. It'll make passing out the trays much easier at snack time. Any extras can feed volunteers and church staff. Our *highly recommended* maximum Crew size is six–5 Crew members and one leader–which means 3 cups of granola per brown paper bag.

Snack Time

When all the Climbing Crews have arrived and found a place to sit, use your Yak Bell to get everyone's attention. Welcome Crews to Mountaintop Treats, and invite today's snack service Crews to join you up front. Lead everyone in a round of applause and thanks for their work in preparing today's snack.

Hold up your sample snack, and describe how it is a reminder of the Bible verse and of God's strong, sweet comfort. Explain that everyone who wants granola can spoon it on top of the yogurt. Tell Crew Leaders they'll use the "Today's Mountaintop Treat" cards to continue talking about today's Bible focus.

Remind everyone to have clean hands and to have Prayer Persons lead their Crews in a prayer of thanks for the snack before they eat. Finally, have the snack service Crews serve the trays of snacks and cups of water and your kitchen crew deliver any trays prepared for allergy restrictions.

Finishing Up

When you hear your VBS Director's signal, ask Crews to help by putting their plates, cups, and napkins in the trash containers. Then dismiss kids to their next station.

Your kitchen crew can help pick up the Crew mats or blankets, wipe up any spills (if you're eating indoors), and straighten up the kitchen and snack area before they leave. Share a round of high fives for a successful day at Mountaintop Treats!

Day 2

Today's Mountaintop Treat

Rock Rambler's Parfait

Read aloud today's Bible verse: **"He comforts us in all our troubles so that we can comfort others" (2 Corinthians 1:4).** Ask:

- **What about God's power to comfort shows us that God is strong?**
- **What are ways God's comfort is also sweet or gentle?**

Say: **Both foods in our snack can comfort growling tummies. The yogurt is soft and sweet, kind of like God's gentle comfort. The granola is tough and even looks a little like rocks! God has the power to comfort *(Hold on!)* and helps us stay strong. When God shows us his gentle and strong comfort, it can help us comfort others.**

Hey! Remember to use the Bible Buddy app! Snack is a great time to bring the Bible focus to life on your smart device!

Available on the App Store | ANDROID APP ON Google play

Day 2

Today's Mountaintop Treat

Rock Rambler's Parfait

Read aloud today's Bible verse: **"He comforts us in all our troubles so that we can comfort others" (2 Corinthians 1:4).** Ask:

- **What about God's power to comfort shows us that God is strong?**
- **What are ways God's comfort is also sweet or gentle?**

Say: **Both foods in our snack can comfort growling tummies. The yogurt is soft and sweet, kind of like God's gentle comfort. The granola is tough and even looks a little like rocks! God has the power to comfort *(Hold on!)* and helps us stay strong. When God shows us his gentle and strong comfort, it can help us comfort others.**

Hey! Remember to use the Bible Buddy app! Snack is a great time to bring the Bible focus to life on your smart device!

Available on the App Store | ANDROID APP ON Google play

Permission to photocopy this resource from Group's Everest VBS granted for local church use. Copyright © 2015 Group Publishing, Inc., Loveland, CO. group.com/vbs

DAY 3

Bible Story: God heals Naaman. (2 Kings 5)

Bible Point: God has the power to heal.

Key Verse: "He heals the brokenhearted and bandages their wounds." (Psalm 147:3)

Did You Know?

- Naaman is described in 2 Kings 5:1 as having leprosy. Most Bible scholars agree there are two general types of leprosy described throughout Scripture. The first type is known today as Hansen's disease and is what most people associate with the word "leprosy"—a contagious disease that disfigures the body and leads to an early death. The other reference to leprosy in Scripture describes more general skin diseases that, while significant, were less severe conditions—although there was still a social stigma connected with them. Because Naaman's condition is not described as being contagious, he probably had this second, less severe type of leprosy.
- To assist Naaman in seeking a cure for his leprosy, the king of Aram (Syria) sent Naaman with an introduction letter and gifts to present to the king of Israel. These gifts included 750 pounds of silver and 150 pounds of gold. That amount is astounding! Today that many pounds of silver and gold would be worth around three-quarters of a *billion* dollars!
- Second Kings 5:17 says that Naaman took two loads of earth (soil) back home with him after he had been healed. In ancient Middle-Eastern culture, the identity of a god was often associated with the land where they were worshiped. Naaman took the soil back to Aram as a tangible reminder of what God had done for him; Naaman most likely would have used the soil to build an altar to God.

Why It Matters...

Today's kids are used to instant gratification. Computers, smartphones, and tablets help kids connect with friends, information, and the world around them in seconds. As you talk about God's power to heal, you have the opportunity to remind kids that God's healing doesn't usually happen instantly. Sometimes healing can take a long time, whether it's a broken bone, an illness like cancer, or the healing of a relationship. And sometimes healing doesn't happen until we're in heaven with God. Help kids understand God's power to heal and the many different ways that healing may come.

At Everest VBS, the daily Bible Point is carefully integrated into each station's activities for unforgettable Bible learning. See how your station reinforces today's Bible Point.

DAY 3

God has the power to heal.

Base Camp Sing & Play

- Learn the Day 3 Bible Point and key verse, and meet Bible Memory Buddy Mallory.
- Sing Everest VBS songs.
- Discuss God Sightings, and hang a God Sightings Flag.
- Trek got his new climbing crew sick, and now he's trying to heal them in a hurry!

Bible Expeditions

- Dip seven times in the Jordan River, and watch their spots disappear.

Mountaintop Treats

A Heart-y Snack

KidVid™ Cinema

When Cole's dad got really sick, Cole and his brothers had to hold on to God's mighty power

Imagination Station

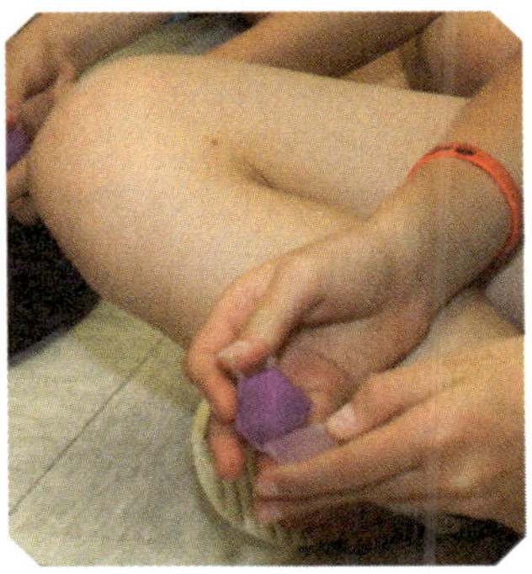

Watch sand "heal" together to become something incredible!

Summit Celebration

- Who's in the spotlight today in Spotlight VBS?
- Review the day.
- Get the day's Bible Bands to take home.
- Cover hurts with a big bandage prayer.

Glacier Games

Say What?

Getting Warm

Climbing Team Chase

Day 3

Supplies

- ▲ fresh strawberries (2 whole strawberries per participant)
- ▲ plain rice cakes (1 per participant)
- ▲ whipped cream cheese (8-ounce container per Crew)
- ▲ honey or maple syrup (3 to 4 ounces per Crew)
- ▲ electric mixer and large mixing bowl
- ▲ kitchen knife and cutting board
- ▲ large paper plates (5 per prep table plus 1 per VBS Crew)
- ▲ small paper plates (1 per participant at snack time)
- ▲ plastic knives (5 per prep table plus 1 per participant at snack time)
- ▲ medium-size bowls to hold ice (1 per Crew)
- ▲ large bags of cubed ice (1 per 10 Crews)
- ▲ photocopies of "Today's Mountaintop Treat: A Heart-y Snack" (1 per Crew)

Allergy Alert!

If there are children with food allergies, find out what parts of today's snack are okay for them to eat. Prepare any necessary snack variations or alternatives in advance. For the Crews with allergy alerts, you can prepare those Crews' entire tray with the snack variation to ensure there aren't any mix-ups of who gets what snack and no one feels left out. Be sure to carefully check ingredient lists, as some food is made in facilities that also process peanuts.

Today's Treat—A Heart-y Snack

This scrumptious, crunchy treat provides a look at one way God has the power to heal.

Before Snack Service Crews Arrive

Wash strawberries thoroughly, and cut leaves away with a triangle cut. Then cut the strawberries into ⅛-inch slices. The slices should resemble heart shapes. Slice 25 heart-shapes for each Crew at your VBS and divide the slices into one bowl or plate for each prep table for your snack prep Crews to finish.

Empty the whipped cream cheese from all of the containers into a large mixing bowl (you'll reuse the containers), and add 3 to 4 tablespoons of honey per container of cream cheese. Starting on a low speed with the electric mixer, blend the cream cheese and honey and whip until smooth. Then transfer portions of the mixture back into a cream cheese container for each Crew, and place all into a refrigerator.

For a nondairy option, replace the whipped cream cheese with Silk Vanilla Soy Fruity & Creamy yogurt. You can find honey cream cheese in stores, but it often contains nuts. If you'd like to purchase premade honey cream cheese, read the label carefully to avoid possible allergy issues.

Fill bowls with ice to keep the cream cheese chilled, one bowl per prep table. Place supplies at each prep table. You'll need five large paper plates at each prep table for prep Crews to work on. You'll also need one large paper plate per Climbing Crew: divide the total for your VBS among the prep tables. Make sure each prep table has wet wipes and paper towels for hand cleaning. Make a completed sample snack.

Welcome to Snack Service

After all the snack service Crews have gathered, use the Yak Bell to get their attention.

Say: **Welcome to the Mountaintop Treats kitchen. Today's *your* day to make a yummy snack for all the Climbing Crews here at Everest VBS! And when everyone comes to eat, you'll get to serve the snacks you've made. It's fun to work in the kitchen and make a Mountaintop Treat, but it also feels really good to serve others!**

The Bible Connection

Say: **Each day, our snack reminds all of us about our special Bible verse. Today's verse says, "He heals the brokenhearted and bandages their wounds" (Psalm 147:3).** Hold up your sample snack. **Today we'll get supplies ready for everyone to make one of these snacks. Everyone will get to put strawberry pieces together to look like hearts being put back together. It'll be a great reminder about the way God can heal our hurting hearts from feeling sad, scared, or lonely to help us feel happy, loved, and not alone.**

Briefly explain to kids what they'll do during snack assembly by following the steps on the next page. Everyone can work together to complete each step.

Have children clean their hands thoroughly with wet wipes before and after making the snacks. These treats require a lot of handling—so be sure Crew Leaders remind kids to keep fingers out of their mouths while they work!

Snack Assembly

1. Use a plastic knife to cut each heart-shaped strawberry slice in half—so the new slices look like half of a heart shape. Continue until all strawberry slices have been cut down the center into two pieces.

2. Place 50 strawberry heart halves onto a paper plate for each snack tray.

3. Count out and stack six rice cakes for each snack tray.

4. For each snack tray, include a bowl of ice and a container of the honey whipped cream cheese. Place the containers of cream cheese on top of the ice to keep them chilled for snack time. (Station Leader: You can put these back in the refrigerator for the time between snack prep and snack time, if you like.)

5. Place 6 plastic knives, 6 paper plates (these can be stacked under the plate with the strawberry slices), 6 napkins, and a copy of the "Today's Mountaintop Treat" handout on each tray.

Snack Blessing

Have the Prayer Person for each snack service Crew ask God to bless the snacks they've just prepared for others at Everest VBS.

Snack Time

When all the Climbing Crews have arrived and found a place to sit, use your Yak Bell to get everyone's attention. Welcome everyone to Mountaintop Treats. Invite the snack service Crews to join you up front, and lead everyone in a round of applause and cheers of thanks for their work on today's snack.

Explain how the snack connects to the Bible verse and reminds us of the way God can heal our hurt or broken hearts.

Say: **When you get your snack food, you can spread the cream cheese frosting on your rice cake. Then, Crew Leaders, you'll use your Mountaintop Treat card to guide the rest of your snack activity and continue talking about today's Bible focus. There should be enough strawberry slices for each person in your Crew to put together four hearts on your rice cake.**

Remind everyone to have clean hands before they eat. Have the Prayer Persons lead their Crews in a prayer of thanks for the snack. Then have the snack service Crews serve the trays and cups of water. Your kitchen crew can deliver any trays prepared for allergy restrictions.

Finishing Up

When you hear your VBS Director's signal, ask Crews to help by putting their cups and napkins in the trash containers. Then dismiss kids to their next station.

Your kitchen crew can help pick up the Crew mats or blankets, wipe up any spills (if you're indoors), and straighten up the kitchen and snack area before they leave. Shout with cheerful hearts for another successful day at Mountaintop Treats!

Day 3

Today's Mountaintop Treat

A Heart-y Snack

Read aloud today's Bible verse: **"He heals the brokenhearted and bandages their wounds" (Psalm 147:3).**

Say: **When we get well after feeling sick or sad, it's a *good* feeling! Kind of like our heart is happy and whole.** Hold two strawberry slices together so they look like a whole heart. As your Crew puts strawberry heart halves together on rice cakes and starts eating, work together to make up a song to celebrate that **God has the power to heal. *(Hold on!)*** You can make up your song to the tune of well-known songs such as "Mary Had a Little Lamb" or "Twinkle, Twinkle Little Star." Once you've made up a song, sing it to a Crew next to you.

Hey! Don't forget to use the Bible Buddy app! I'll help you bring the Bible to life on your smart device!

Available on the App Store | ANDROID APP ON Google play

Day 3

Today's Mountaintop Treat

A Heart-y Snack

Read aloud today's Bible verse: **"He heals the brokenhearted and bandages their wounds" (Psalm 147:3).**

Say: **When we get well after feeling sick or sad, it's a *good* feeling! Kind of like our heart is happy and whole.** Hold two strawberry slices together so they look like a whole heart. As your Crew puts strawberry heart halves together on rice cakes and starts eating, work together to make up a song to celebrate that **God has the power to heal. *(Hold on!)*** You can make up your song to the tune of well-known songs such as "Mary Had a Little Lamb" or "Twinkle, Twinkle Little Star." Once you've made up a song, sing it to a Crew next to you.

Hey! Don't forget to use the Bible Buddy app! I'll help you bring the Bible to life on your smart device!

Available on the App Store | ANDROID APP ON Google play

Bible Story:
Jesus dies on a cross to take away our sins, then comes back to life.
(Luke 22:31–24:12)

Bible Point:
God has the power to forgive.

Key Verse:
"You are a God of forgiveness."
(Nehemiah 9:17)

DAY 4

Did You Know?

- The Romans reserved crucifixion—a cruel, painful, and slow way to die—for criminals without Roman citizenship. Usually only slaves, rebels, and the worst political offenders received such a gruesome sentence. This horrible public punishment was meant to deter crime throughout the empire.
- After being cruelly beaten, Jesus was forced by guards to carry one of the beams of the cross, a common practice in Bible times. Jesus carried this beam about a third of a mile, and the wood beam could have weighed as much as 125 pounds.
- Luke is the only book of the Gospels that tells about Jesus forgiving the thief. Jesus tells the thief, "I assure you, today you will be with me in paradise" (Luke 23:43). The word *paradise* is only used three times in the New Testament. (It's also in 2 Corinthians 12:4 and Revelation 2:7). Some scholars believe the word refers to a place of rest between death and resurrection.
- When Jesus died on the cross, the curtain in the inner sanctuary of the Temple was torn in two. This inner space, the Holy of Holies, was the earthly dwelling place of God's presence. God ordained that only the high priest could go past this curtain once a year. The torn curtain revealed that now, because of Jesus' sacrifice, anyone who puts their faith in Jesus has access to God.

Why It Matters...

Jesus lived a perfect life and was wrongly put to death. Everyone who witnessed Jesus' death knew a great injustice had taken place. Jesus didn't deserve to die, but he still forgave the people who crucified him! Today help kids understand that because of Jesus' sacrifice on the cross, we have been forgiven for our sins too. Share with kids the wonderful news that there is nothing they can do to make God love them less and nothing they can do that God won't forgive them for. God is able to forgive us an infinite amount of times—he is the ultimate forgiver!

DAY 4

God has the power to forgive.

At Everest VBS, the daily Bible Point is carefully integrated into each station's activities for unforgettable Bible learning. See how your station reinforces today's Bible Point.

Base Camp Sing & Play

- Learn the Day 4 Bible Point and key verse, and meet Bible Memory Buddy Pike.
- Sing Everest VBS songs.
- Discuss God Sightings, and hang a God Sightings Flag.
- Trek isn't sure his new crew will forgive him. What if they miss their chance to climb Mount Everest?

Bible Expeditions

- Visit with Peter, place their fingerprints on a cross, and know that God forgives them.

Mountaintop Treats

Summit Sponge Cake

KidVid™ Cinema

Philip shares how he had to forgive his little brother Timothy for breaking a special, treasured toy.

Imagination Station

Watch the Leapin' Blizzards fly high, just like our hearts do when we experience forgiveness.

Summit Celebration

- Enjoy today's Spotlight VBS.
- Review the day.
- Get the day's Bible Bands to take home.
- Find out how Jesus picks up the pieces of broken relationships with the power of forgiveness.

Glacier Games

Nobody's Perfect

Yak Relay

Sharing Forgiveness

Pretzel rods dipped in white almond bark & rolled in blue sprinkles then formed into a cross & they look like an icicle

Day 4

Graham cracker sheet, frosting, Skittles or M&M's to make cross

Today's Treat—Summit Sponge Cake

Today's snack will remind kids that Jesus died on a cross to wipe away our sins and that God has the power to forgive.

Before Snack Service Crews Arrive

Wash the berries, and fill a bowl for each prep table with a mix of blueberries and raspberries. Place the bowls on the prep tables, along with the other supplies. Make sure each prep table has wet wipes and paper towels for hand cleaning. Slice a piece of angel food loaf cake about 1 inch thick as an example for the snack service Crews.

Welcome to Snack Service

After all the snack service Crews have gathered, use the Yak Bell to get their attention.

Say: **Welcome to the Mountaintop Treats kitchen! Today *you* get to put together the snack ingredients that'll feed our hungry climbers at Everest VBS. When everyone comes to eat, you'll get to serve the snacks you've made. It's fun to make the snacks, but it feels even better to take care of others!**

Supplies

- angel food loaf cakes (1 per Crew)
- blueberries—fresh or thawed from frozen (5 per participant)
- raspberries—fresh or thawed from frozen (5 per participant)
- Cool Whip or similar whipped topping (8-ounce container per Crew)
- plastic knives (5 per prep table)
- medium-size bowls (1 per prep table)
- plastic spoons (1 per Crew)
- resealable sandwich bags (1 per participant)
- plastic forks (1 per participant)
- small plastic plates (1 per participant)
- large paper plates (5 per prep table plus 1 per VBS Crew)
- Tide to Go pens (optional)
- photocopies of "Today's Treat: Summit Sponge Cake" (1 per Crew)

Trail Tip

Cool Whip used to be listed as a nondairy whipped topping, but it contains casein that can be problematic for people with dairy allergies. You can find soy-based whipped topping at health food stores and divide the container into bowls for the Crews that need a dairy-free option.

Allergy Alert!

If there are children with food allergies, find out what parts of today's snack are okay for them to eat. Prepare any necessary snack variations or alternatives in advance. For the Crews with allergy alerts, you can prepare those Crews' entire tray with the snack variation to ensure there aren't any mix-ups of who gets what snack and no one feels left out. Be sure to carefully check ingredient lists, as some food is made in facilities that also process peanuts. You can find gluten-free angel food cake mixes in health food stores and prepare those a day ahead or use gluten-free cinnamon raisin bread as a snack alternative.

The Bible Connection

Say: **Each day, our snack helps us remember our special Bible verse. Today's verse tells us some wonderful things about God. It says, "You are a God of forgiveness" (Nehemiah 9:17).**

We have a good, loving, forgiving God, and that's a *big* deal because every person in the entire world needs God's forgiveness. We all sin—that means we all do wrong sometimes—but God sent his Son, Jesus, to wipe away the mess our sins make.

Hold up the slice of angel food cake. Let kids guess what it is and what it will be used for in today's snack. **We get to do something special with these "cake sponges" today during snack that will help us remember what Jesus did for us—you'll learn more about that in Bible Expeditions and Summit Celebration. Let's get started on our snack-making!** Briefly explain the snack assembly steps. Kids can choose to cut angel food cake or put berries into resealable plastic bags.

Have children clean their hands thoroughly before and after making the snacks. These treats smell and taste delicious—so be sure Crew Leaders remind kids to use hand wipes to keep fingers clean while they work and to wait until snack time to eat!

Snack Assembly

1. Count 5 blueberries and 5 raspberries into each resealable bag. Crew Leaders can help seal the bags and make sure the air is pressed out of each bag as it's sealed.

2. Slice the loaves of angel food cake. Crew Leaders can cut the first slice about an inch thick as a guide for all the slices.

3. Place six slices of angel food cake on a large paper plate for each Climbing Crew tray.

4. Place 6 bags of berries, 1 spoon, 6 plastic forks, 6 napkins, 6 small plastic plates (tucked under the paper plate with the angel food cake slices), a container of whipped topping, and a copy of the "Today's Mountaintop Treat" handout on each tray.

Snack Blessing

Have the Prayer Person for each snack service Crew ask God to bless the snacks they've just prepared for others at Everest VBS.

Field Test Finding

During field test, we realized that paper plates soaked up too much of the berry juice and didn't leave very much for the angel food cake during the snack activity. Plastic plates won't steal away the yummy juice and will make the activity more visually impacting!

Snack Time

When all Climbing Crews have arrived and found a place to sit, use your Yak Bell to get everyone's attention. Welcome everyone to Mountaintop Treats, and have the snack service Crews join you up front for a big round of applause and thanks for their hard work.

Sound the Yak Bell again, if needed, to get everyone's full attention. Tell Crew Leaders that snack time will be a little different today, and ask them to wait for instructions once their snack tray is delivered. Have the snack service Crews pass out the trays and cups of water, and have your kitchen crew deliver trays prepared with allergy modifications.

Say: **Crew Leaders, allow each Crew member to take a plastic bag of berries. Make sure everyone's bag is sealed and doesn't have air trapped in it—so it won't pop.** Pause. **Being careful not to tear your bag, everyone can squish the berries to make a berry juice mess! As you're making a mess, talk with your Crew members about wrong things we can say and do—those are sins—like lying, taking things that don't belong to us, or being mean to someone.** Allow a few minutes for Crew members to work.

Now everyone *carefully* pour out your berries and juice onto a plate and slide a slice of angel food cake over the top of the berry mess to soak up the juice. Crew Leaders, help spoon some whipped topping in the shape of a cross on top of each cake slice. As we eat our sweet treats, let's remember that Jesus' life and death shows us God has the power to forgive. *(Hold on!)*

Crew Leaders will use the "Today's Mountaintop Treat" cards to continue talking about today's Bible focus. Remind everyone to have clean hands before they eat. Have the Prayer Persons lead their Crews in a prayer of thanks for the snack.

Field Test Finding

We kept Tide pens on hand just in case anyone got blueberry or raspberry juice on clothing during snack prep and snack time—but we didn't have to use them! Kids loved the sensory activity of squishing the berries in the plastic bags, and the fun, juicy mess stayed contained.

Finishing Up

When you hear your VBS Director's signal, ask Crews to help by putting their sandwich bags, plates, spoons, and napkins in the trash containers. Then dismiss kids to their next station.

Your kitchen crew can help pick up the Crew mats or blankets, wipe up any spills (if you're eating indoors), and straighten up the kitchen and snack area before they leave. Share a round of high fives for another great day at Mountaintop Treats and to celebrate the way Jesus solved the problem of our sin mess!

Day 4

Today's Mountaintop Treat

Summit Sponge Cake

Read aloud today's Bible verse: **"But you are a God of forgiveness" (Nehemiah 9:17).**

Say: **Every person in the world does wrong sometimes—everyone sins, and it can leave our lives a mess.** Point to the berry juice on your slice of cake and say: **God sent his perfect Son, Jesus, to die on a cross to wipe away—take the punishment for—our sins.** Point to the whipped-topping cross. Ask:

? **What are ways we can show Jesus thanks for what he did for us?**

Hey! Remember to use the Bible Buddy app! Snack is a great time to bring the Bible focus to life on your smart device!

Available on the App Store | Android app on Google play

Day 4

Today's Mountaintop Treat

Summit Sponge Cake

Read aloud today's Bible verse: "But you are a God of forgiveness" (Nehemiah 9:17).

Say: Every person in the world does wrong sometimes—everyone sins, and it can leave our lives a mess. Point to the berry juice on your slice of cake and say: God sent his perfect Son, Jesus, to die on a cross to wipe away—take the punishment for—our sins. Point to the whipped-topping cross. Ask:

? What are ways we can show Jesus thanks for what he did for us?

Hey! Remember to use the Bible Buddy app! Snack is a great time to bring the Bible focus to life on your smart device!

Available on the App Store | Android app on Google play

DAY 5

Bible Story: Jesus promises us an eternal home. (John 14:1-3)

Bible Point: God has the power to love us forever.

Key Verse: "Everyone who believes in him will have eternal life." (John 3:15)

Did You Know?

- Jesus described heaven as a house filled with many rooms, an expression meaning unlimited space. So we know heaven is really big—big enough for everyone who believes in Jesus!
- Jesus gave his disciples this message of comfort and the assurance of heaven to help prepare them for what was ahead. He knew the disciples would soon face many trials and persecutions, beginning with his own betrayal, trial, and crucifixion.
- Jesus mentioned heaven many, many times in the Gospels. But he didn't give many details of what heaven is like. This is because Jesus was more concerned with making sure people knew *how* to spend eternity with him—by believing in him! "I am the way, the truth, and the life. No one can come to the Father except through me" (John 14:6).
- Jesus used parables often during his ministry to explain truths to his followers. But during his last night with the disciples, described in John 13-17, Jesus spoke very plainly. This was Jesus' last chance to make sure the disciples understood who he was, the work he had for them, that he would have a place waiting for them in heaven, and that he would one day return to earth!

Why It Matters...

Sometimes the Bible can seem like a big history book filled with stories from a long, long time ago. But our God is not a character in a story from once upon a time. God always has been and always will be—he is forever! Use today's lesson to help kids discover the hope they have in a heavenly future. Share the excitement Jesus' followers have and the unimaginably wonderful forever home we have waiting for us in heaven.

At Everest VBS, the daily Bible Point is carefully integrated into each station's activities for unforgettable Bible learning. See how your station reinforces today's Bible Point.

DAY 5

God has the power to love us forever.

Base Camp Sing & Play

- Learn the Day 5 Bible Point and key verse, and meet Bible Memory Buddy Yeddy.
- Sing Everest VBS songs.
- Discuss God Sightings, and hang a God Sightings Flag.
- Trek is geared up and ready to summit Mount Everest! Finally!

Bible Expeditions

- Enjoy earthly comforts, and then talk about how cool heaven will be!

Mountaintop Treats

Pizza Peaks

KidVid™ Cinema

Olivia and Elyse tell what it was like to trust God as they prayed for their uncle to know and love God.

Imagination Station

Puzzle out the solution to the Befuddler, and explore the joy of sharing God's power with others.

Summit Celebration

- Watch the adorable preschoolers in today's Spotlight VBS.
- Review the day.
- Get the day's Bible Bands to take home.
- Figure out what lasts forever!

Glacier Games

Always Go, Go, Going!

Icy Pass

Loopy Volley

Tortille Chips + Salsa

- Triangle sugar cookies w/ frosting snow
- watermelon triangles w/ whipped cream top

Day 5

Supplies

- pita bread (4 whole rounds per Crew) or gluten-free triangular crackers
- pizza sauce (about 8 ounces per Crew)
- shredded mozzarella cheese (about 8 ounces per Crew)—nondairy options can be found at most grocery stores
- large bowls (2 per prep table)
- scooping spoons (5 per prep table)
- plastic knives (5 per prep table)
- plastic spoons (1 per participant at snack time)
- disposable bowls (2 per Crew at snack time)
- resealable sandwich bags (1 per participant)
- paper plates (5 per prep table plus 1 per participant at snack time)
- photocopies of "Today's Mountaintop Treat: Pizza Peaks" (1 per Crew)

Today's Treat—Pizza Peaks

Today's snack is a fun way to review the Bible Points of the week and reinforce today's Point, God has the power to love us forever.

Before Snack Service Crews Arrive

Cut a sample pita bread triangle to place at each prep table for Crews to use for reference. There's a handy guide for you below.

Pour pizza sauce into large bowls, one per prep table, and divide the mozzarella cheese into large bowls, one per prep table. Set the bowls of pizza sauce and cheese, sample pita triangles, and other supplies on each prep table. Make a completed snack as an example.

Welcome to Snack Service

After all the snack service Crews have gathered, use the Yak Bell to get their attention.

Say: **Welcome to snack service here in the Mountaintop Treats kitchen! Today *you* finally get to jump into the treat-making fun. And later, when everyone comes to eat, you'll get to serve the snacks you've made. It's fun to make the snacks, but it also feels really good to serve others.**

Allergy Alert!

If there are children with food allergies, find out what parts of today's snack are okay for them to eat. Prepare any necessary snack variations or alternatives in advance. For the Crews with allergy alerts, you can prepare those Crews' entire tray with the snack variation to ensure there aren't any mix-ups of who gets what snack and no one feels left out. Be sure to carefully check ingredient lists, as some food is made in facilities that also process peanuts.

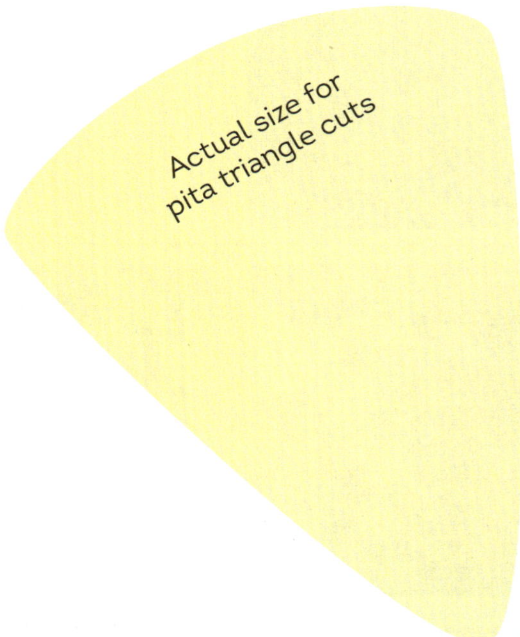

The Bible Connection

Say: **Each day at Everest VBS, our snack has reminded us of our special Bible verse. Today's verse is an amazing promise from God: "Everyone who believes in him will have eternal life" (John 3:15). An eternal life means a forever life.** Ask:

In your Climbing Crew, tell what you think *forever* means.

Allow a minute for Crews to discuss. Sound the Yak Bell to get everyone's attention, and then invite a few willing kids to share answers.

Say: **This week we've been on an awesome climb up Mount Everest, and today we're at the peak! We made it!** Lead kids in a cheer to celebrate. **Our journey up this mountain is coming to an end, but our journey with God can go on *forever.* When we love God and his Son, Jesus, we can have a forever life with God in heaven. Now that's an adventure!**

Today's snack (hold up your completed snack sample) **will remind us of reaching the peak at Everest VBS** (point to the tip of your sample snack) **and that our journey with God doesn't end at a peak but can keep going and going and *going.*** Briefly explain the snack assembly steps. Everyone can work together to complete each step.

Have children clean their hands thoroughly with wet wipes before and after making the snacks. Crew Leaders can also remind kids to keep fingers clean and out of their mouths while they work!

Snack Assembly

1. Cut pita bread slices in half with plastic knives.

2. Slice pita bread halves into four triangular pieces. It's best to cut from the straight edge toward the rounded edge to make the triangle shapes.

3. Put five triangle pieces of pita bread into each resealable bag.

4. Spoon pizza sauce and shredded cheese into two disposable bowls for each Crew tray.

5. Place 1 bowl of pizza sauce, 1 bowl of cheese, 6 bags of pita triangles, 6 spoons, 6 napkins, 6 paper plates (these can go under the bags of pita triangles) and a copy of "Today's Mountaintop Treat" on each serving tray.

Snack Blessing

Have the Prayer Person for each snack service Crew ask God to bless the snacks they've just prepared for others at Everest VBS.

Snack Time

When all the Climbing Crews have arrived and found a place to sit, use your Yak Bell to get everyone's attention. Welcome everyone to Mountaintop Treats. Invite the snack service Crews up front with you for a round of applause and a thank you from the other Crews.

Say: **Our snack today is called Pizza Peaks. For each of your triangle "peaks," you'll add pizza sauce and then sprinkle some cheese on the point to look like a snow-capped peak. Let's use our snack to help us remember all the things we've learned about our powerful God this week.**

Crew Leaders will use the "Today's Mountaintop Treats" card to connect the snack with the Bible verse and talk about each day's Bible Point. Remind everyone to have clean hands before they eat. Have the Prayer Persons lead their Crews in a prayer of thanks for the snack. Then have the snack service Crews serve the snacks and cups of water. Have your kitchen crew serve any trays prepared with allergy modifications.

Finishing Up

When you hear your VBS Director's signal, ask Crews to help by putting their used disposables in the trash containers. Then dismiss kids to their next station.

Your kitchen crew can help pick up the Crew mats or blankets, wipe up any spills (if you're indoors), and straighten up the kitchen and snack area before they leave. Share a round of high fives for an awesome week of Everest VBS Mountaintop Treats!

Day 5

Today's Mountaintop Treat

Pizza Peaks

Read aloud today's Bible verse: **"Everyone who believes in him will have eternal life" (John 3:15).** Ask:

? **What excites you about the forever home God's made in heaven for everyone who loves him?**

Say: **As we make each of our yummy Pizza Peaks, let's see if we remember all the true things we learned about our powerful God this week.** As kids add the pizza sauce and cheese to each pita triangle, invite your Crew to tell what they've learned about each day's Bible Point.

Day 1: God has the power to provide.
Day 2: God has the power to comfort.
Day 3: God has the power to heal.
Day 4: God has the power to forgive.
Day 5: God has the power to love us forever.

Remember your Bible Buddy app! Choose me, your pal Yeddy, to bring today's Bible verse to life.

Available on the App Store | ANDROID APP ON Google play

Day 5

Today's Mountaintop Treat

Pizza Peaks

Read aloud today's Bible verse: "Everyone who believes in him will have eternal life" (John 3:15). Ask:

? What excites you about the forever home God's made in heaven for everyone who loves him?

Say: As we make each of our yummy Pizza Peaks, let's see if we remember all the true things we learned about our powerful God this week. As kids add the pizza sauce and cheese to each pita triangle, invite your Crew to tell what they've learned about each day's Bible Point.

Day 1: God has the power to provide.
Day 2: God has the power to comfort.
Day 3: God has the power to heal.
Day 4: God has the power to forgive.
Day 5: God has the power to love us forever.

Remember your Bible Buddy app! Choose me, your pal Yeddy, to bring today's Bible verse to life.

Available on the App Store | ANDROID APP ON Google play

Permission to photocopy this resource from Group's Everest VBS granted for local church use. Copyright © 2015 Group Publishing, Inc., Loveland, CO. group.com/vbs